Get Over It!

A Winning Skills Book by
JOY BERRY

Artwork by
Bartholomew

GOLD STAR
PUBLISHING

SuperstarKids.com

CREDITS

Senior Editor	Marilyn Berry
Managing Editor	Keith D. Stewart
Project Manager	Jim Wools
Print Production Manager	Joe Cudmore
Copy Editor	Tom McIntyre
Electronic Production	Tonia Farnell, Grace Guerra-Milke, Marty Osckel, Dan Dever
Editorial Consultants	Lisa Berry, Carol Sauder, Mel Sauder

Published by Gold Star Publishing, Inc.

Manufactured in the United States by Bowne of Phoenix

© 1991 & 2000 Joy Berry. All rights reserved.

No part of this publication may be reproduced in whole or in part by any mechanical, photographic, or electronic process, or in the form of an audio, video, or CD recording, nor may it be stored in a retrieval system, or transmitted in any form or by any means, now known or hereafter invented, or otherwise copied for public or private use without the written permission of Joy Berry and Gold Star Publishing, Inc.

For information regarding permission, write to Gold Star Publishing, Inc., P.O. Box 2032, Scottsdale, Arizona 85252-2032.

You can handle tough situations if you know
- what tough situations are,
- the different types of tough situations,
- the various origins of tough situations,
- the six steps for handling tough situations that you create,
- the six steps for handling tough situations that you did not create, and
- the things that make it easier to handle tough situations.

4 ■ WHAT TOUGH SITUATIONS ARE

A tough situation is one that jeopardizes someone's happiness or well-being.

> MY PARENTS GROUNDED ME BECAUSE I LIED TO THEM. NOW I CAN'T GO TO BASEBALL PRACTICE FOR A WEEK.

> BUT THAT MEANS THAT YOU WON'T BE ABLE TO PITCH IN SATURDAY'S GAME!

WHAT TOUGH SITUATIONS ARE ■ 5

A tough situation can hurt you or someone else.

6 ■ DIFFERENT TYPES OF TOUGH SITUATIONS

Some tough situations can cause **physical harm**.

> THE WORST SITUATION I EVER FACED WAS THE TIME I WENT HIKING WITH SOME FRIENDS. WE WERE LOST FOR OVER 24 HOURS. THE TEMPERATURE DROPPED AND WE NEARLY FROZE TO DEATH!

DIFFERENT TYPES OF TOUGH SITUATIONS ▪ 7

Some tough situations can cause **mental or emotional harm.**

8 ■ DIFFERENT TYPES OF TOUGH SITUATIONS

Short-term tough situations last for a short period of time such as an hour or a day.

> ONE OF THE WORST SITUATIONS I EVER FACED, HAPPENED AT A PARK. THE CHILD I WAS BABYSITTING WANDERED AWAY WHILE I WAS TAKING HIS SISTER TO THE RESTROOM. LUCKILY, A POLICE OFFICER FOUND THE CHILD AND BROUGHT HIM BACK TO ME.

DIFFERENT TYPES OF TOUGH SITUATIONS ▪ 9

Long-term tough situations last for a long period of time such as several days, weeks, or months.

10 ■ DIFFERENT TYPES OF TOUGH SITUATIONS

Whether a tough situation is short-term or long-term, it seldom disappears automatically.

DIFFERENT TYPES OF TOUGH SITUATIONS ■ 11

In fact, a tough situation that is not handled appropriately can become worse and possibly can create additional tough situations.

12 ■ ORIGINS OF TOUGH SITUATIONS

To handle a tough situation appropriately, it is important to determine who or what created it.

Sometimes *you* create a tough situation by breaking a natural law.

A *natural law* is a specific principle established by nature.

ORIGINS OF TOUGH SITUATIONS ■ 13

When you break a natural law, you often experience the negative consequences that automatically occur when the law is broken.

This puts you in a tough situation.

14 ■ ORIGINS OF TOUGH SITUATIONS

Sometimes *you* create a tough situation by breaking a man-made law.

A **man-made law** is a rule established by people.

ORIGINS OF TOUGH SITUATIONS ■ 15

When you break a man-made law, you often are forced to pay a penalty that is imposed on you by the people who enforce the law.

This puts you in a tough situation.

16 ■ ORIGINS OF TOUGH SITUATIONS

Common sense is good judgement that is based on simple logic and reasoning.

Sometimes you create a tough situation by disregarding your common sense and acting against it.

ORIGINS OF TOUGH SITUATIONS ▪ 17

When you act against your common sense, you often experience the negative consequences that automatically occur when you do something that is illogical and senseless.

18 ■ ORIGINS OF TOUGH SITUATIONS

Natural circumstances beyond your control are occurrences, caused by nature, that you cannot prevent or change.

ORIGINS OF TOUGH SITUATIONS ■ 19

Sometimes natural circumstances beyond your control create tough situations.

Human circumstances beyond your control are occurrences, caused by other people, that you cannot prevent or change.

ORIGINS OF TOUGH SITUATIONS ■ 21

Sometimes human circumstances beyond your control can create tough situations.

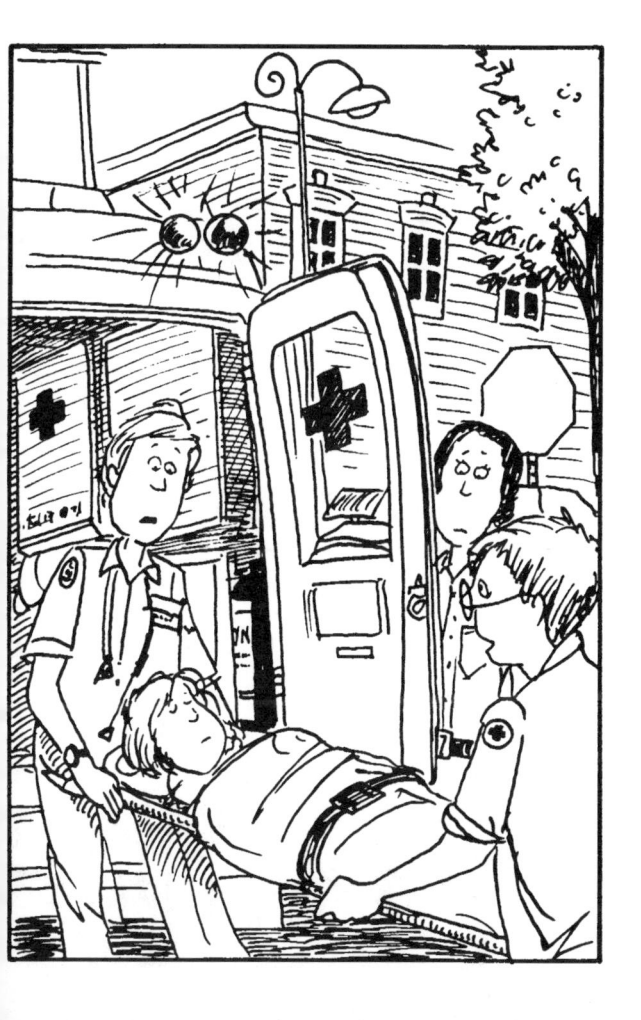

22 ■ SIX STEPS FOR HANDLING TOUGH SITUATIONS YOU CREATE

Here are six steps for handling tough situations that *you* create:

Step 1: Face it.

Admit that you are experiencing a tough situation. Do not pretend that everything is OK.

SIX STEPS FOR HANDLING TOUGH SITUATIONS YOU CREATE ■ 23

Step 2: Accept it.

Accept this fact: The tough situation is not going to go away automatically. Realize that you are going to have to put time and effort into resolving it.

24 ■ SIX STEPS FOR HANDLING TOUGH SITUATIONS YOU CREATE

Step 3: Think about it.

Find out the answers to these questions:

- What did I do to create this situation?
- What consequences will I have to experience?

> I LOST AMY'S JACKET, SO I'M GOING TO HAVE TO FACE HER AND ADMIT WHAT I'VE DONE. SHE'LL PROBABLY BE PRETTY MAD AT ME, BUT I'M JUST GOING TO HAVE TO TAKE IT.

SIX STEPS FOR HANDLING TOUGH SITUATIONS YOU CREATE ■ 25

Step 4: Decide what to do.

Find out the answers to these questions:

- What do I need to do to make the people I may have hurt feel better?
- What do I need to do to make myself feel better?

Make sure that the things you decide to do are not harmful to yourself or to others.

26 ■ SIX STEPS FOR HANDLING TOUGH SITUATIONS YOU CREATE

Step 5: Do what you have decided to do.

If you have hurt other people, you need to do what you can to make them feel better. Make sure that you
- admit that you have done something wrong,
- say that you are sorry,
- do whatever you can to make up for your wrongdoing (make sure that your efforts are acceptable to the people you have hurt), and
- try not to do the same thing again.

SIX STEPS FOR HANDLING TOUGH SITUATIONS YOU CREATE ■ 27

You also need to make yourself feel better. Make sure that you
- remember that you are a human being (you are not perfect, and it is normal for you to make mistakes),
- forgive yourself when you do something that is wrong,
- learn whatever you can from the situation, and
- try not to do the same thing again.

28 ■ **SIX STEPS FOR HANDLING TOUGH SITUATIONS YOU CREATE**

Step 6: Talk about your thoughts and feelings.

A tough situation can cause you to have many thoughts and feelings that should not be ignored. Pay attention to them. Share them with someone else. When you talk to someone, you need to make sure that the person is

- someone who you respect and can trust,
- someone who cares about you, and
- someone who is old enough and wise enough to help you.

SIX STEPS FOR HANDLING TOUGH SITUATIONS YOU CREATE ■ 29

Talking about a tough situation one time will probably not make everything OK. Therefore, you need to continue to talk about your thoughts and feelings for as long as you feel a need to do so.

30 ■ STEPS FOR HANDLING TOUGH SITUATIONS YOU DID NOT CREATE

Here are six steps for handling tough situations that you did *not* create:

Step 1: Face it.

Admit that you are experiencing a tough situation. Do not pretend that everything is OK.

Step 2: Accept it.

Accept this fact: The tough situation is not going to go away automatically. Realize that you are going to have to put some time and effort into resolving it.

32 ■ STEPS FOR HANDLING TOUGH SITUATIONS YOU DID NOT CREATE

Step 3: Think about it.

Find out the answers to these questions:

- What happened to create this tough situation?
- What is going to happen to me?

STEPS FOR HANDLING TOUGH SITUATIONS YOU DID NOT CREATE ■ 33

Step 4: Decide what to do.

Find out the answers to these questions:

- What can I do to make the situation better?
- What can I do to make myself feel better?
- What can I do to make the other people who are involved in this situation feel better?

Step 5: Do what you have decided to do.

If possible, you should
- talk to the people who created the tough situation (if you cannot talk to them, talk to someone else),
- try to understand why these people did what they did,
- try to forgive them,
- do not blame yourself in any way, and
- do whatever you can to make yourself and the other people involved in the situation feel better.

> I REALIZE THAT HISTORY IS A TOUGH SUBJECT FOR YOU, SO I CAN UNDERSTAND WHY YOU WOULD WANT ME TO WRITE YOUR TERM PAPER. BUT WHAT YOU'RE ASKING ME TO DO ISN'T FAIR! IT WOULD TAKE A LOT OF WORK, AND IT MIGHT GET ME IN TROUBLE. SO WHAT I PROPOSE IS THAT I TELL YOU STEP-BY-STEP HOW TO WRITE A PAPER AND THEN YOU DO IT YOURSELF...

STEPS FOR HANDLING TOUGH SITUATIONS YOU DID NOT CREATE ■ 35

Step 6: Talk about your thoughts and feelings.

It is important that you continue to talk over your thoughts and feelings about the tough situation until you feel better.

36 ■ HANDLING TOUGH SITUATIONS

It will be easier to handle a tough situation if you are calm.

A good way to calm yourself is to
- stop whatever you are doing,
- take several deep breaths and let them out slowly, and
- relax your body.

HANDLING TOUGH SITUATIONS ▪ 37

Here is one way to relax your body:

- Slowly count to ten.
- Tense your entire body more and more with each count. By the time you reach 10, your body should feel completely tense from your head to your toes.
- Slowly count backwards from ten.
- Relax your entire body more and more with each count. By the time you reach 10, your body should feel completely relaxed all over.

38 ■ HANDLING TOUGH SITUATIONS

It will be easier to handle a tough situation if you slow down your thoughts and focus them on dealing with the situation.

HANDLING TOUGH SITUATIONS ■ 39

Avoid doing anything that will cloud your thinking.

This includes using substances such as alcohol or non-prescription drugs to calm yourself.

40 ■ HANDLING TOUGH SITUATIONS

It will be easier to handle a tough situation if you remember these six facts:

Fact #1. There are some good things about every situation. Try not to focus on the bad things about a situation. Instead, look for the good things and focus your attention on them. This will help prevent you from becoming so depressed that you cannot deal appropriately with the situation.

Fact #2. Things could always be worse. Try to realize that no matter how bad a situation seems to be, it could always be worse. Be thankful that it is not worse. Being thankful will help you to feel better.

42 ▪ HANDLING TOUGH SITUATIONS

Fact #3. Every problem has a solution. When a tough situation creates problems for you, try not to waste your time and energy feeling bad about them. Instead, realize that there are solutions to your problems. Spend your time and energy finding the solutions. This will help you to overcome the problems and to feel better.

HANDLING TOUGH SITUATIONS ■ 43

Fact #4. Every person can find the solutions to his or her problems. Remember that every person has the ability on their own or with the help of others, to find the solutions to any problem. Realizing this will help prevent you from giving up before your problems are resolved.

Fact #5. "This too shall pass." Remember that just as every experience has a beginning, it also has an ending. This includes any tough situation that you encounter. Realizing this can make it easier for you to endure difficult times.

HANDLING TOUGH SITUATIONS ■ 45

Fact #6. "Time heals all wounds." Remember, by handling tough situations in a positive way, the pain you experience most likely will fade with the passing of time. Realizing this can make it easier for you to endure difficult times.

46 ■ CONCLUSION

Tough situations do not have negative endings automatically.

CONCLUSION ■ 47

Tough situations can have positive endings if they are handled appropriately.

Tough situations that are handled appropriately can help you to grow and to become a better person.